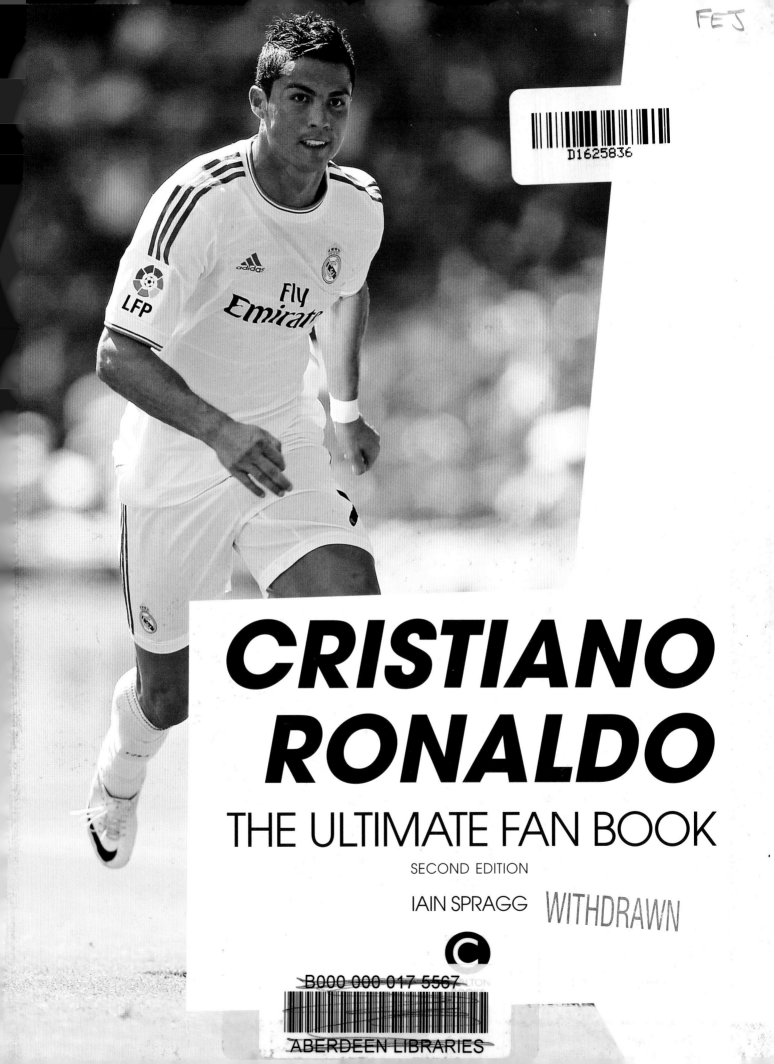

CRISTIANO RONALDO

THE ULTIMATE FAN BOOK

SECOND EDITION

IAIN SPRAGG

CONTENTS

Right: Ronaldo's goals against Sweden in the playoffs for the finals of the 2014 FIFA World Cup ensured Portugal travelled to Brazil.

INTRODUCTION

From his early years on the Portuguese island of Madeira to becoming a superstar in Madrid, the story of Cristiano Ronaldo's career is an incredible footballing blockbuster.

Cristiano Ronaldo is the most famous footballer on the planet and thanks to his record-breaking performances in the red of Manchester United and the white of Real Madrid, he is now regarded as the game's greatest player.

The Portuguese magician is football's ultimate showman and no one can match the explosive entertainment he provides on the pitch. Watching Ronaldo is a masterclass in how to destroy the opposition – in style!

Worshipped by his millions of fans and feared by every team he plays against, Ronaldo has come a long way since he joined his first team in his hometown of Funchal as a young boy and began his journey to fame and fortune. It has been a remarkable rise and on the way he has lit up every pitch he has played on with his incredible skills.

The Real Madrid star has won every major club trophy in England and Spain, as well as the UEFA Champions League and FIFA World Club Cup – and there's still lots more to come from him.

He is already Portugal's top scorer of all time, a Spanish league record-breaker in front of goal and a three-time winner of the Ballon D'Or, the award given each year to the world's best player.

Cristiano Ronaldo: The Ultimate Fan Book is a celebration of the genius of the Portuguese striker and his amazing achievements. It takes you on a journey that starts in Madeira, passes through Lisbon and Manchester up to his arrival at Madrid's Bernabeu stadium, at which he has become the world's greatest player.

The book also looks at Ronaldo's life away from football, his family and his fame, as well as how hospital surgery helped him overcome a heart problem as a teenager.

You don't have to be a Manchester United or Real Madrid supporter to love Ronaldo's unique talents and this book is the ultimate guide to the ultimate player.

Above: Ronaldo displays another of the trademark tricks that have made him a global superstar.

Below: No-one has scored more international goals for Portugal than the Real Madrid hero.

Above: In front of his adoring Real Madrid fans, Ronaldo shows off the 2013 Ballon d'Or as FIFA World Footballer of the Year.

THE EARLY YEARS

The Real Madrid star was an unruly pupil at school!
But away from the classroom it was obvious he had a
very special talent.

Ronaldo was born on February 5, 1985 on the Portuguese island of Madeira. He was christened Cristiano Ronaldo dos Santos Aveiro by his parents because his father, José, was a big fan of an old Hollywood actor called Ronald Reagan. When Ronaldo was born, Reagan had become President of the USA.

The family lived in the city of Funchal on the south coast of the island. José worked as a gardener for the local council while his mother Maria was a cook. They were not rich but the lack of money only helped to bring Ronaldo and his two older sisters, Elma and Liliana Cátia, and his big brother, Hugo, closer together.

Above: Nine-year-old Ronaldo's identity card for the 1994–95 season, when he played for Clube Futebol de Andorinha in Funchal, Madeira.

Above: Ronaldo grew up in a poor family but enjoyed a happy childhood on the Portuguese island of Madeira.

"I was brought up with nothing," Ronaldo said. "We were very poor. I had no toys and no Christmas presents. I shared a room with my brother and two sisters and my parents slept in the other. It was a small space but I didn't mind. I'm incredibly close to my brother and two sisters and we loved being together. For us it was normal, it was all we knew. Everybody around us lived the same way and we were happy."

When he was eight years old, Ronaldo joined the junior team at his local club, Andorinha. But while his first football coaches were amazed by his skills, his school teachers were not as impressed. "I was not thick but I was not interested in school," he said. "I was expelled after I threw a chair at the teacher. He disrespected me. When I got to 14 ... I thought I was maybe good enough at that time to play semi-professionally."

His family agreed with him and decided that he should concentrate on his football rather than his studies. Ronaldo was now on his way to becoming the world's greatest footballer.

Below: Since signing for Real Madrid, Ronaldo has become the game's greatest player.

THE NEXT STEPS

The superstar began to make a big impression in his home country of Portugal, despite a frightening problem with his health.

Ronaldo spent two seasons with Andorinha but it was already obvious that the boy was a special talent. So in 1995 he switched clubs, joining Nacional, in his hometown of Funchal. He was still only 10 years old but this move had a big effect on his career.

In his first season at Nacional, Ronaldo's Under-11 team won their league title and word was beginning to spread about the team's skinny midfielder with the outrageous skills. "People knew I was a talented kid," Ronaldo said.

The talent spotters at big club Sporting Lisbon, based in Portugal's capital city, had heard of him and he was invited to the club for a three-day trial. It meant leaving the island of Madeira and heading to the Portuguese mainland but Ronaldo was determined to take his big chance. After the trial, Sporting Lisbon decided to offer him an apprenticeship.

Ronaldo continued to impress the coaching staff at Sporting, but at the age of 15 he was suddenly diagnosed with a serious heart problem and the club decided he needed an operation to cure it.

The problem was that his heart was beating too fast, even when he wasn't running. His mother Maria said, "The people in charge at Sporting called me and I went to Portugal where I had to sign some papers so he could be treated in hospital. I was worried because he might have to give up playing football. But the treatment went well and after a few days he was back training again."

Luckily, Ronaldo make a complete recovery and starred for Portugal at the European Under-17 Championship held in Denmark in 2002, starting in the group games against France and Ukraine. When he got back to his club, he was promoted to the reserves. So the teenager had almost made it to the first team and a few months later took the final step to become a full senior player.

Above: From his first days at Sporting Clube de Portugal (aka Sporting Lisbon), Ronaldo took his pre-training stretching exercises very seriously.

Below: Sporting's fans, especially at their Estádio José Alvalade home, are among Portugal's most passionate.

Above: Even in training, Ronaldo was all business because he knew that perfecting his technique would take him a long way.

HIS BIG BREAKTHROUGH

Just a few months after his 17th birthday, Ronaldo made the headlines with a sensational league debut for Sporting Lisbon.

Although everyone in Lisbon knew just how talented Ronaldo was, he was not yet well known outside the city. But all that changed in October 2002 when the teenager was given his senior debut for the club.

The Sporting manager, Laszlo Boloni, decided Ronaldo was ready to perform with all the top professionals and put him in the team to play against Moreirense in a Portuguese Primeira Liga game at the club's home ground, the Estádio José Alvalade.

The time had come for Ronaldo to show the world his magic and the 17-year-old did not disappoint. Sporting won the match – and Ronaldo scored twice!

His first goal came in the first half after he picked up the ball inside the Moreirense half and set off on an amazing run. His speed took him past one sliding tackle and when a second player closed in on him, he produced an outrageous stepover which left the embarrassed defender behind him. The Moreirense goalkeeper rushed out but Ronaldo did not panic and unleashed a deadly low shot which hit the back of the net.

His second goal came in second-half injury time. Sporting were awarded a free-kick near the corner flag and as the ball came sailing into the area, it was Ronaldo who jumped above the Moreirense defence to head home and seal the team's 3–0 victory.

Above: Five months after his 17th birthday, Ronaldo saw first-team action for Sporting Lisbon in preseason friendlies.

A star had been born. Every football fan in Portugal had now heard of the youngster from Madeira and his life would never be the same again.

Ronaldo made 24 more Primeira Liga appearances for his club during the 2002–03 season as Sporting finished third in the table. He also scored twice in three Portuguese Cup games. He was suddenly the hottest property in Portuguese football and although he didn't yet realise it, it would not be long before one of the most biggest and famous clubs in the world was knocking on Sporting's door trying to sign the teenager.

Above: A month after his first-team debut for Sporting, Ronaldo was showing off his ball skills to Maritimo defenders Albertino (left) and Joel.

MOVING TO ENGLAND

After just one full season with Sporting, Ronaldo was on his way to Old Trafford to play for the mighty Manchester United.

It was not long after Ronaldo's amazing debut for Sporting that some of Europe's top clubs began to take notice of the teenager. Both Liverpool and Barcelona were interested and Ronaldo even met Arsenal manager Arsene Wenger at the club's training ground to discuss joining the Gunners.

The race for his signature was hotting up but there could only be one winner – Manchester United.

What really sealed the deal was a friendly between Sporting and United in the summer of 2003 in Lisbon. The game was staged to celebrate the opening of Sporting's new stadium and Ronaldo was the man of the match as his Portuguese team beat the Premier League champions 3–1.

Six days later United signed him for £12.24 million, handing the 18-year-old the number seven shirt worn by David Beckham the previous season. Manager Sir Alex Ferguson admitted it was Ronaldo's dazzling display in the friendly in Portugal that convinced him he was going to become a star.

"He is an extremely talented footballer, a two-footed attacker who can play anywhere up front," Ferguson said after the deal was done. "After we played Sporting last week the lads in the dressing room talked about him constantly and on the plane back from the game they urged me to sign him. That's how highly they rated him. He is one of the most exciting young players I've ever seen."

It was the start of a brilliant six seasons for Ronaldo in England in which he won eight major trophies, was voted the best player in Europe in 2008 and scored more than 100 goals for the Red Devils. Old Trafford worshipped their Portuguese playmaker and Ronaldo repeatedly repaid the fans with some of the most magical football they had ever seen.

Above: Ronaldo takes the ball away from Nicky Butt in summer 2003; within a week they were Manchester United team-mates.

Below: Ronaldo in UEFA Champions League action for Manchester United, taking on Porto's Maniche in 2003.

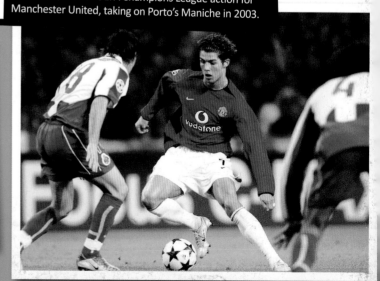

"He surpassed all the other great ones I coached at Manchester United. And I had many."

Sir Alex Ferguson

Above: Ronaldo celebrates another goal for United, helping them to knock out FC Porto in the 2008–09 UEFA Champions League quarter-final.

NEW NATIONAL HERO

Football is Portugal's number one sport and in Ronaldo the country has a special player to make the nation proud.

Before Ronaldo burst onto the scene more than 10 years ago, the two most famous names in the history of Portuguese football were two players called Eusebio and Luis Figo. Both were amazing flair players who won all the big trophies at club level and gave some incredible performances for the national team.

Ronaldo however has eclipsed them both and is now recognised as the greatest player Portugal has ever produced.

It all began when the then Sporting Lisbon star was given his international debut as a teenager in a friendly match against Kazakhstan in 2003. He played for just 45 minutes, but he was in the starting line-up for his second cap two months later when Portugal smashed Albania 5–3. It was already obvious Portugal had unearthed a new hero.

Above: Cristiano Ronaldo was just 18 when he won his first cap for Portugal against Kazakhstan in 2003.

His first full 90 minutes of action came during Euro 2004 and the dramatic penalty shootout win over England in Lisbon in the quarter-finals. Although Portugal were ambushed in the final by Greece, Ronaldo was now a firm fixture in the team.

Left: Ronaldo was on target during the 2004 Olympic Games against Morocco.

Since then the striker has surpassed both Eusebio and Figo and rewritten the Portuguese record books.

In November 2011, Ronaldo equalled Figo's brilliant haul of 32 international goals with two strikes against Bosnia-Herzegovina in a Euro 2012 qualifier. He matched and then went past Eusebio's record of 41 goals when he scored a superb hat-trick over Northern Ireland in a World Cup qualifier in September 2013.

The Real Madrid marksman long ago sailed past Eusebio's milestone of 64 international appearances, and although Figo is still Portugal's most capped player with 127 caps, Cristiano now has 120 caps to his name, and it won't be long before he breaks that record, too.

Ronaldo is now the joint Portuguese record holder for appearances at the World Cup with 11, and for goals scored at the European Championships, where he has netted six times. He also jointly holds the record for the most matches played at the European Championships, with 14.

The Portugal legend still has several years left to play, so there's no doubt he will one day become his country's record holder for everything!

Above: Back at the Estadio José Alvalade, where he first made his name, Ronaldo scores Portugal's opening goal in their 2–1 semi-final defeat of the Netherlands at Euro 2004.

WORLD CUP STAR

Having played in three World Cups – in Germany in 2006, South Africa in 2010 and Brazil in 2014 – Ronaldo is one of international football's biggest stars.

It is every player's dream to play in the World Cup and Ronaldo has already done it three times with Portugal, displaying his dazzling skills to TV audiences right around the world. The Madrid magician was born to play in football's most famous event.

It was Ronaldo's seven goals in qualifying that booked Portugal's place in the 2006 World Cup. They were unbeaten on their way to the Finals and went on to win Group D as Ronaldo scored from the spot in the 2–0 victory over Iran.

Inspired by Ronaldo's attacking play, everyone was talking about Portugal as potential World Cup winners, and when they beat Holland 1–0 in the Last 16, there was real hope that the team could go all the way.

England stood in their way in the quarter-finals, but the match was scoreless so a penalty shootout beckoned. It fell to Ronaldo to take the all-important final kick and he kept his cool superbly to send keeper Paul Robinson the wrong way and win the match.

But although the semi-final against France brought heartbreak, as Zinedine Zidane scored the only goal of the game to knock Portugal out, Ronaldo and his nation's performances were recognised when they were given the FIFA award for the Most Entertaining Team.

Above: Ronaldo scored the winner for Portugal against Ghana at the 2014 World Cup.

In 2008, Ronaldo was made Portugal captain at the age of just 23, only two months before the start of qualifying for the 2010 World Cup in South Africa. He rose to the challenge brilliantly and steered his team safely to the Finals.

Portugal were drawn in a tough group that had both Brazil and the Ivory Coast in it, but Ronaldo made sure they reached the knockout stages, scoring Portugal's seventh and final goal in their 7–0 demolition of North Korea in Cape Town. European champions Spain were the opposition in the last 16, but despite trying his luck with two trademark free-kicks, Ronaldo could not stop Portugal losing 1–0.

Portugal were back in World Cup action in 2014 thanks to four Ronaldo goals in qualifying and four more that destroyed Sweden in the play-offs, but despite his 50th international goal in the group game against Ghana, the Portuguese narrowly missed out on qualification for the knockout phase on goal difference.

Left: Ronaldo celebrates after helping Portugal to knock out England in the 2006 FIFA World Cup quarter-final.

Below: Ronaldo dances past Brazilian defender Juan during the goalless draw in the group stage of the 2010 FIFA World Cup in South Africa.

GREAT MANCHESTER UNITED GOALS

Ronaldo hit an incredible 118 goals in England in just 292 appearances for the mighty Manchester United. These are five of his very best…

MANCHESTER UNITED 2 *PORTSMOUTH 0*
PREMIER LEAGUE, JANUARY 30, 2008

Ronaldo is the most deadly player in the world with a long-range free-kick and this sensational 30-yard effort at Old Trafford was one of his very best. It flew like a laser-guided missile past Portsmouth keeper David James and into the top right corner of the net.

MANCHESTER UNITED 4 *ASTON VILLA 0*
PREMIER LEAGUE, MARCH 29, 2008

A beautiful goal that few other players could have dreamed of scoring, Ronaldo pounced on a loose ball in the penalty area and then cheekily back-heeled the ball behind his left leg, through a crowd of confused defenders and into the back of the net.

CHELSEA 1 MANCHESTER UNITED 1
CHAMPIONS LEAGUE, MAY 21, 2008

The best players always save their best for the very biggest matches and Ronaldo did the business in the UEFA Champions League Final in Moscow when he rose above the Chelsea defence to punch home Wes Brown's cross with a thumping header. United went on to win the trophy after a penalty-shootout.

Above: Ronaldo blasts the ball towards goal to give Manchester United a 1–0 win over FC Porto in the UEFA Champions League quarter-final.

Above: Rising high above the watching Chelsea defence, Ronaldo heads Manchester United's goal in the 2008 UEFA Champions League Final.

PORTO 0 *MANCHESTER UNITED 1*

CHAMPIONS LEAGUE, APRIL 15, 2009

United need to win to reach the semi-finals of the Champions League and Ronaldo delivered when it mattered most with a truly spectacular winner, a thunderbolt from 40 yards out that almost burst the net as it screamed past the stunned Porto keeper. Even Ronaldo's team-mates could not believe what they had just seen.

ARSENAL 1 *MANCHESTER UNITED 3*

CHAMPIONS LEAGUE, MAY 5, 2009

Another utterly unstoppable free-kick, Ronaldo unleashed this magnificent effort against Arsenal in the Champions League semi-final, blasting home from a wide angle past the wall and beating Gunners' keeper Manuel Almunia for pace and power at his near post.

MANCHESTER UNITED MILESTONES

Above: Ronaldo shows off the FA Cup after he had scored the opening goal of the 2004 final against Millwall, a match United won 3–0.

AUGUST 16, 2003
Ronaldo makes his debut for Manchester United, coming off the bench to replace Nicky Butt after 61 minutes in a 4–0 demolition of Bolton Wanderers at Old Trafford.

MAY 22, 2004
Scores the opening goal in a 3–0 win over Millwall in the FA Cup Final to lift his first piece of silverware with the Red Devils. He went on to win three Premier League titles (2006–07, 2007–08, 2008–09), two League Cups (2006 and 2009), the Champions League (2008) and the FIFA Club World Cup (2008) with United.

AUGUST 9, 2005
Scores the third goal in a 3–0 victory for United in their UEFA Champions League qualifier against Hungarian side Debrecen, his first-ever goal in Europe.

APRIL 1, 2007
Ronaldo is named the Football Writers' Association Footballer of the Year. He had already been voted the PFA Young Player, Players' Player and Fans' Player of the Year and became the first footballer ever to hold all four awards at the same time.

MARCH 19, 2008
Captains Manchester United for the first time in his career at the age of 23, scoring both of the goals in the Red Devils' comfortable 2-0 victory against Bolton Wanderers at Old Trafford.

Above: The Portuguese star was just 23 years old when he was voted European Footballer of the Year and received the UEFA Ballon d'Or.

NOVEMBER 15, 2008
Scores his 100th United goal in a 5–0 thrashing of Stoke City.

MAY 11, 2008
Scores in a 2–0 victory away at Wigan. It's his 31st Premier League goal of the season, a feat which earned him the European Golden Shoe award.

DECEMBER 2, 2008
Ronaldo collects the Ballon D'Or for the first time, the award given to the best footballer in Europe, beating Lionel Messi into second place in the vote.

JANUARY 12, 2009
Ronaldo becomes the first Premier League player ever to be voted FIFA World Player of the Year.

MAY 10, 2009
Scores in a 2–0 defeat of Manchester City at Old Trafford, his 118th and final goal for United in 292 appearances for the club.

DECEMBER 22, 2009
Collects the first-ever FIFA Puskas Award for the best goal of the year, his 40-yard thunderbolt against FC Porto in the UEFA Champions League.

REAL MADRID MILESTONES

Above: Thousands of Real Madrid fans, and another Portuguese legend Eusebio, were at the Estadio Barnabeu to welcome Ronaldo to the club.

JULY 1, 2009
Joins Real Madrid from Manchester United for world-record fee of £80 million.

APRIL 20, 2011
Scores the winner in extra-time of the Copa del Rey Final against Barcelona to lift his first trophy as a Madrid player.

MAY 21, 2011
Scores twice in an 8–1 demolition of Almeira in the final league game of the season. His double strike takes his tally for the season to 40, the first player in La Liga history to reach this number.

MAY 2, 2012
The striker finds the back of the net in a 3–0 away win against Athletic Bilbao, a result which gives Real Madrid the Spanish league title for a record-breaking 32nd time. He wins the La Liga player of the season.

MAY 13, 2012
Scores in a 4–1 league victory against Real Mallorca, a goal which makes Ronaldo the first player in the history of La Liga to score against every other team in the division in a single season.

MAY 8, 2013
Scores 200th goal for the club, against Malaga, to reach a double-century of strikes quicker than any of the other great players in the history of the club.

JANUARY 13, 2014
Ronaldo picks up the FIFA Ballon D'Or award for the world's best footballer for the second time.

Above: Ronaldo celebrates after scoring one of his five goals in the 9–1 victory over Grenada in La Liga on April 5, 2015.

MAY 24, 2014
Ronaldo scores in the 4–1 win over Atletico Madrid in the UFEA Champions League final. His 17th goal in 11 appearances breaks the previous Champions League/European Cup single-season record of 14.

AUGUST 12, 2014
Scores twice in Real Madrid's 2–0 victory over Sevilla in the UEFA Super Cup.

AUGUST 28, 2014
Wins UEFA Best Player in Europe award.

JANUARY 14, 2015
Wins the Ballon d'Or for the third time.

MARCH 10, 2015
Scores two goals in Real's 3–4 home defeat to Schalke in the Champions League to become the outright top scorer in all UEFA competitions (with 78 goals) and joins Lionel Messi as the Champions League's all-time top scorer.

APRIL 5, 2015
Scores five goals in one game for first time in professional career (including a nine-minute hat-trick) in a 9–1 victory over Granada in La Liga.

MAY 2, 2015
Scores 29th hat-trick of Real Madrid – against Sevilla – to break Alberto di Stefano's club record.

AT HOME WITH RONALDO

When he's not showing off his unbelievable skills on the pitch, Ronaldo enjoys a quiet life away from the spotlight.

It's not easy being one of the most famous people on the planet and Ronaldo gets away from the pressures of playing for Real Madrid by spending his free time with family and friends. He became a father in July 2010 when Cristiano Ronaldo Junior was born and the star insists there is nowhere he would rather be than at home with his son.

"I am a very private person and I am down-to-earth," he said. "My family comes first — my son is the most important thing in my life. I salute him in the crowd every time I score a goal. After that it's the football that matters most to me. Money comes after that."

One thing that has always marked out Cristiano as a special player is his absolute dedication to football. He would much rather stay at home, looking after himself, than go out with his Bernabeu team-mates.

"Half the boys like to go to the disco. They like to party hard, they like to try to impress girls with champagne. But it's better to train hard and do well."

Ronaldo's father sadly died in 2005 but he remains very close to his mother, his sisters and his brother and despite all the money he earns, he is not that interested in cash.

"I bought my mother a £400,000 house in Portugal," he said. "She lives there with her partner and my son. I bought my sisters houses as well. My brother runs my nightclubs and various bars. I also own a hotel. But money hasn't changed me — I'm still the same person. I have my circle of friends, my club. People who've been with me a long time. I look after these people."

Ronaldo is a devout Roman Catholic and believes his religion has helped him to become such a remarkable success on the pitch.

"I collect crucifix necklaces because of my relationship with God," he said. "I always had a gift. I was shown the skills and I am a fantastic footballer but I do believe God gave me the gift."

Right: Despite his massive fame and fortune, Ronaldo has always remained incredibly close to his mother Maria.

"I always had a gift. I was shown the skills and I am a fantastic footballer but I do believe God gave me the gift."

Below: Ronaldo poses with his son beneath a statue of himself during the unveiling ceremony in his hometown in Funchal in December 2014.

Above: The Portuguese legend, receiving the 2013 FIFA Ballon d'Or from Pele, spends as much time as possible with his young son Cristiano.

27

PLAYING IN THE EUROS

Ronaldo was just 18 years old when he made his international debut and has now starred at three European Championships for Portugal.

Ronaldo first played for his country in August 2003, when he came off the bench against Kazakhstan. His Manchester United debut had come only four days before, against Bolton Wanderers, and was the start of an exciting new phase of his incredible career.

Less than a year later he was playing in Euro 2004, which was held in Portugal, and, although he was still only a teenager, Ronaldo was in amazing form as the hosts went all the way to the Final.

His goal in the semi-final win over Holland was crucial and despite Portugal losing in the Final to Greece, Ronaldo was named in the UEFA All-Star Team of the competition alongside star names like Zinedine Zidane, Frank Lampard, Michael Ballack and fellow Portuguese Luis Figo.

Above: Ronaldo celebrates after scoring against the Czech Republic in the 2008 European Championship finals.

Ronaldo scored an incredible seven goals in the qualifying matches as Portugal reached Euro 2008 in Switzerland and Austria. For the first time, he was handed the number seven shirt for a big tournament by manager Luiz Felipe Scolari.

A goal and a man-of-the-match performance in a 3–1 group stage win over the Czech Republic sent Portugal safely through to the knockout phase but even Ronaldo could not stop Germany beating his side in the quarter-finals.

Ronaldo's third appearance in the European Championships came in 2012 in Poland and Ukraine

Left: Ronaldo's first major tournament for Portugal was Euro 2004.

and Portugal went into their final group game against Holland needing a win to stay in the tournament. Step forward Ronaldo with two goals to save the day.

He was on target again with the only goal of the game against the Czech Republic in the quarter-finals. But there was heartbreak in the semi-final against Spain as Portugal lost on penalties. However, Ronaldo had shown his superstar status and was again named in the UEFA Team of the Tournament.

His next chance at European glory will come in 2016 when an expanded European Championship kicks off in France. Ronaldo came so close to glory in 2004 and he will be desperate to get his hands on the famous trophy when the tournament is staged again.

Below: Ronaldo terrorises Spain with a trademark dribble during the Euro 2012 semi-final in Donetsk.

GREAT REAL MADRID GOALS

The Portuguese has been deadly in front of goal since he signed for Real Madrid in 2009 and here are five of his most spectacular efforts...

VILLAREAL 0 **REAL MADRID 2**
LA LIGA, SEPTEMBER 23, 2009

Ronaldo's blistering pace was incredible as he spun away from a desperate Villareal tackle on the halfway line and raced towards goal. His speed took him past another attempted tackle before he fired home into the bottom right corner.

REAL MADRID 6 VILLAREAL 2
LA LIGA, FEBRUARY 21, 2010

Even with his reputation for amazing free-kicks, few expected the Portuguese star to score against Villareal as he carefully placed the ball 35 yards out from goal. But he, of course had other ideas, launching a dazzling drive from the left that sailed beautifully into the top right corner.

RAYO VALLECANO 0 **REAL MADRID 1**
LA LIGA, FEBRUARY 26, 2012

A wonder goal worthy of winning any game, there seemed no danger when Rayo cleared a Real corner and Ronaldo was forced to retreat away from goal with the ball. Cue an outrageous, deadly back-heel that completely surprised the Vallecano defenders and keeper.

Above: Ronaldo is congratulated by Marcelo after his brilliant goal at Villareal's Madrigal in September 2009.

Right: Ronaldo's amazing back-heel against Rayo Vallecano in 2012 was simply world class.

REAL MADRID 2 BARCELONA 1
SPANISH SUPER CUP, AUGUST 29, 2012

The highlight of this remarkable goal was the amazing back-heel flick in the middle of the pitch over Gerard Pique that left the Barcelona defender stranded before Ronaldo smashed an unstoppable drive past Victor Valdes to win the Spanish Super Cup.

REAL MADRID 3 GRANADA 0
LA LIGA, SEPTEMBER 2, 2012

The Portuguese's second in this La Liga clash was amazing, racing through the middle of the Granada defence to collect Jose Callejon's pass. His first effort was saved by the keeper but Ronaldo was first to the loose ball, cheekily flicking home with his left foot.

Below: Ronaldo finishes off the fantastic move against Barcelona with the winner in 2012 Spanish Super Cup.

Above: Ronaldo's second goal against Granada in September 2012 showcased his blistering pace as well as speed of thought.

SUPER SKILLS

Ronaldo's amazing array of tricks and awesome talents are what makes him the world's greatest player

IN THE AIR

Loads of Ronaldo's goals come from headers and there are few players who can jump as high or hang in the air as long before he thumps home another headed effort. The power he is able to generate with his snap headers is awesome.

FABULOUS FLIP FLAP

One of the most outrageous tricks in his box, Ronaldo's "Flip Flap" gives defenders sleepless nights. First he moves the ball away with the outside of his boot and when the defender makes his move, he rolls his studs over the ball and in the blink of an eye shifts it back with his instep and away from the tackle.

NEED FOR SPEED

Ronaldo is blessed with incredible speed and his ability to race past players anywhere on the field is one of the big reasons he is such a handful. Only the very quickest defenders can live with him.

SUPERB SHOOTING

His long-range shooting is so good that every time he gets past the halfway line, the alarm bells start ringing for defenders. Ronaldo can hit a devastating range of shots, from the inswinger and the flat drive to the outswinger and the dipper.

FANTASTIC FREE-KICKS

Ronaldo has rewritten the rule book when it comes to free-kicks and there's almost no distance from which he can't go for goal. No one can get as much dip and swerve on the ball as the Portuguese but he also has the raw power needed to blast it past the keeper.

DAZZLING DRIBBLING

Speed alone is not enough to make a world-class player and it is Ronaldo's incredible dribbling at full speed that sets him apart. He bamboozles defenders with his unbelievable balance and ability to keep the ball just inches away from his feet.

THE STEP-OVER

Real Madrid fans have lost count of the number of confused defenders Ronaldo has beaten with his devastating step-over, sending defenders first one way and then the other before racing past them as they desperately try not to fall over.

33

WINNING CHAMPIONSHIPS

Ronaldo has been a key part of every team he has played in both in England and Spain. So he knows all about getting his hands on the most important trophies.

Only the most talented teams get to become league champions and Ronaldo has been the star in four of these sides, winning the Premier League three times in a row with Manchester United and La Liga with Real Madrid.

His first Premier League triumph came in the 2006–07 season. United hadn't won the championship for three years but Ronaldo was determined to put that right and after scoring on the opening day in a 5–1 demolition of Fulham at Old Trafford, there was no stopping him.

He finished the campaign as the Red Devils' top scorer with 17 league goals and Sir Alex Ferguson's side were champions again.

Ronaldo was even more deadly in 2007–08 as United defended their title. It was a close race with Chelsea all the way through the season, but his two priceless goals in a 4–1 defeat of West Ham United and another in a 2–0 victory away against Wigan Athletic in the last two games were enough to see off the Londoners' challenge.

The Portuguese was the league's top scorer with 31 goals and it was no surprise when he was later voted Premier League Player of the Year.

United made it a magnificent hat-trick of titles in 2008–09 and once again Ronaldo was the difference as he again finished top scorer for the club with 18 great goals, more than a quarter of the team's Premier League total. He was definitely now an Old Trafford legend.

Real Madrid were desperate for Ronaldo to bring some of that magic to the Bernabeu after his record £80 million transfer in the summer of 2009 and he delivered just that in the 2011–12 season.

Barcelona had won three La Liga titles in a row but Ronaldo almost single-handedly brought that run to an end with a record-breaking season that saw Real Madrid crowned champions, nine points ahead of their big rivals.

The striker scored an unbelievable 46 times in 38 games – more than a third of Real Madrid's total of 121 La Liga goals. This title allowed Ronaldo to become a member of an exclusive club of players who have won league championships in two different countries.

Right: Ronaldo's 46 goals in 38 La Liga games in 2011–12 saw Real Madrid crowned champions of Spain.

PORTUGAL MILESTONES

AUGUST 20, 2003
Makes debut for Portugal, aged just 18 years and seven months, against Kazakhstan.

JUNE 12, 2004
Scores in Portugal's 2–1 group stage defeat against Greece in Porto, his first international goal.

AUGUST 15, 2004
Scores for Portugal in a 2–1 group stage win over Morocco at the Athens Olympic Games.

JUNE 17, 2006
Ronaldo is on target from the penalty spot in a 2–0 victory over Iran in Frankfurt, his first World Cup Finals goal.

FEBRUARY 6, 2007
Captains Portugal for the first time as the team beat Brazil 2–0 in a friendly at the Emirates Stadium. When Carlos Queiroz is appointed coach in July 2008 Ronaldo becomes the permanent captain.

JUNE 21, 2010
Scores in Portugal's 7-0 thrashing of North Korea to join an exclusive club of players to have scored in two FIFA World Cup Finals.

OCTOBER 16, 2012
By winning his 100th cap in a World Cup qualifier against Northern Ireland, Ronaldo becomes only the third Portuguese player to reach this number of appearances (after Luis Figo and Fernando Couto) and the third-youngest European footballer ever after Germany's Lukas Podolski and Estonia's Kristen Viikmäe to make 100 international appearances.

NOVEMBER 19, 2013
A hat-trick from the Real Madrid star in the second leg of their play-off against Sweden sends Portugal to the 2014 World Cup. The goals take Ronaldo's total for Portugal in 2013 to 10, the best international haul of his career so far.

MARCH 5, 2014
The striker scores twice in a 5–1 friendly victory against Cameroon. It takes him to a total of 49 international goals and makes him Portugal's all-time leading scorer, breaking Pauleta's previous record of 47.

JUNE 26, 2014
The striker scores the winner in the group stage match against Ghana in the 2014 FIFA World Cup in Brazil, the 50th goal of his remarkable international career.

JUNE 13, 2015
Scores third hat-trick of his international career, against Armenia in Yerevan, to take his international tally to 55 goals.

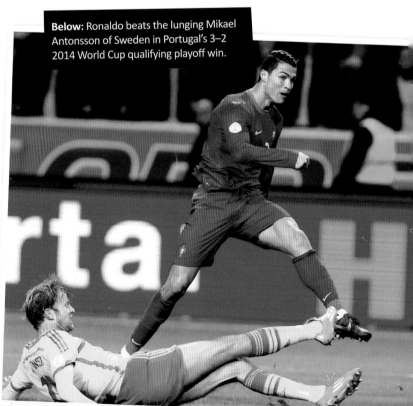

Below: Ronaldo beats the lunging Mikael Antonsson of Sweden in Portugal's 3–2 2014 World Cup qualifying playoff win.

Above: Ronaldo has rewritten the record books while on international duty for his beloved Portugal.

RONALDO IN NUMBERS

Cristiano Ronaldo breaks football records with a regularity that would impress a Swiss clock-maker. Here are some key numbers in the career of the man known as CR7.

Below: Ronaldo has been deadly in front of goal ever since he signed for Madrid.

25.2

The incredible number, in millions, of fans who follow Ronaldo on Twitter.

9

The number of minutes it took the striker to smash three goals past Granada in April 2015, the fastest hat-trick in Real Madrid history.

500

The number of club appearances the Portuguese had made after playing in the Copa del Rey against Barcelona in January 2013.

436

His incredible tally of goals for club (Sporting Lisbon, Manchester United and Real Madrid) and country (Portugal) by the end of the 2014–15 season.

1.17

The average number of goals scored per game by the Real Madrid striker in 2013, an amazing achievement which earned him the famous FIFA Ballon D'Or award.

8

The number of times Ronaldo has been named in the prestigious FIFA FIFPro World XI.

Above: Portugal's captain won his 100th cap for his country against Northern Ireland in 2012.

50,000,000

The number of Facebook "likes" Ronaldo had received by October 2012, the first sportsman to achieve this amount.

2018

The year in which Ronaldo's current contract with Real Madrid will come to an end.

28

The shirt number (which he had worn for Sporting Lisbon) Ronaldo asked for when he signed for Manchester United in 2003. Sir Alex Ferguson refused and told him he would play in the famous number seven.

100

Ronaldo's total number of caps for Portugal after playing in a World Cup qualifier against Northern Ireland in October 2012.

225

The total number of La Liga goals the Portuguese has scored as a Real Madrid player by the end of the 2014–15 season – in only 200 games.

27.99

Percentage of the total vote Ronaldo received to win the FIFA Ballon D'Or in 2013.

29

The number of hat-tricks the star has scored for Real Madrid – breaking Alfredo di Stefano's long-standing club record.

3

The number of times Ronaldo has won the prestigious Ballon d'Or award, given to the world's best player.

9

The number of goals Ronaldo scored in the group stages of the 2013–14 Champions League, a record in the 22-year history of the competition.

TRAINING WITH RONALDO

The Real Madrid star may be blessed with incredible natural talent but he knows that means nothing unless he keeps working hard on the training ground.

Ronaldo was a skinny kid when he arrived at Old Trafford in 2003. The club had just spent £12.24 million on the teenager and although Sir Alex Ferguson and his coaching staff knew he had the skills to become a star, there were question marks about whether he was strong enough to cope with tough English football.

So Ronaldo hit the gym and over the next few seasons spent hours turning himself into a muscular and powerful player. The results were incredible and prove just how seriously he has always taken his training.

But it was not just building muscles that made Ronaldo such a hit at Manchester United. As well as getting stronger, the youngster would spend his spare time watching video clips of football legends like Pele and Johan Cruyff, studying their tricks and techniques so he could make his own game better.

"I am not a perfectionist but I like to feel that things are done well," he once said. "More important than that, I feel an endless need to learn, to improve, to evolve, not only to please the coach and the fans, but also to feel satisfied with myself. It is my conviction that there are no limits to learning, and that it can never stop, no matter what our age."

The striker took his great attitude with him when he signed for Real Madrid and he is famous for staying behind after training sessions to

Above: Practice makes perfect as Ronaldo works on his headers.

Right: Ronaldo warms up with his team-mates ahead of another Real Madrid training session.

practise his trademark free-kicks, constantly working on adding more swerve, dip and power to his shots.

Ronaldo also works very hard in training on his finishing. He will repeat one technique such as a near-post volley or back-post header four times before switching to another way of scoring. It's a way of practising that he learned at Old Trafford and ensures he's always ready when a goal-scoring chance comes along in a match.

"I am not a perfectionist but I like to feel that things are done well... More important than that, I feel an endless need to learn, to improve, to evolve, not only to please the coach and the fans, but also to feel satisfied with myself. It is my conviction that there are no limits to learning, and that it can never stop, no matter what our age."

Above: One of the greatest athletes in the game, Ronaldo is always working to get himself in perfect physical condition.

RONALDO'S SUPERSTAR TEAM-MATES

Although he's the main man at Real Madrid, Ronaldo is surrounded by world-class players at the Bernabeu.

GARETH BALE

Signed from Premier League side Tottenham Hotspur for a world record £85 million in the summer of 2013, the Welsh winger is an amazing natural talent who terrifies defenders with his pace, dribbling ability and eye for goal. Bale's lethal left foot compliments the right-footed Ronaldo beautifully. The deadly duo are capable of ripping apart even the meanest defences in La Liga and Europe.

SERGIO RAMOS

The Spain defender has been part of the Madrid first team since the start of the 2005–06 season and while Ronaldo is scoring goals at one end, it is Ramos's job to stop them at the other. Capped more than 100 times by Spain, Ramos can play at both full-back and in central defence and has won three La Liga titles with the club. Fast, strong and a great reader of the game, he is one of the toughest defenders in world football.

LUKA MODRIC

If Ronaldo is the man who provides the fireworks at the Bernabeu, it is Modric who makes the Madrid midfield tick. Signed from Tottenham Hostpur for £30 million in August 2012, the Croatian maestro initially struggled to find a place in the team under Jose Mourinho, but flourished under the managerial reign of Carlo Ancelotti. His ability to find the perfect pass for Real's frontmen was evident during Real's march to the Champions League crown in 2014.

JAMES RODRIGUEZ

A star of the 2014 World Cup, the Colombian playmaker joined Real for a fee of around €80 million shortly after the tournament, and took little time in proving his status as one of the best No.10s in world football. Injury may have restricted him in his first season at the Bernebeu, but he still contributed 13 goals and 13 assists in 29 appearances, and looks set to be a hero at the Bernebeu for many seasons to come.

RONALDO AND HIS FANS

One of the most popular players on the planet, Ronaldo is worshipped by millions of supporters all over the world.

If you want an idea just how much Real Madrid supporters love their Portuguese superstar, you only need to watch a video of Ronaldo's official unveiling to the fans in 2009. Eighty thousand people packed into the club's Bernabeu stadium to welcome him to Spain.

Most top European clubs don't even get that many supporters for a match, but Ronaldo was so popular in Madrid that there wasn't a spare seat in the ground when he arrived in Spain – before he had even kicked a ball!

The supporters rushed to buy Real Madrid shirts with Ronaldo's name and number nine on the back (since 2010 he has worn the number seven) and just nine months later the club had sold an unbelievable 1.2 million shirts in Madrid alone. That equalled over £80 million worth of sales, more than it cost the club to sign the player from Manchester United!

By the end of 2014, Ronaldo shirts were the best-selling replica shirts in the world, beating Barcelona's Lionel Messi into second place.

There are hundreds of unofficial Ronaldo fan clubs across the world and he is one of the most popular people on social media. An astonishing 37.2 million

Above: The Madrid superstar is a heartthrob as well as a football hero.

fans follow him on Twitter and by August 2015 he had received an astonishing 104.9 million "Likes" on his Facebook page.

In December 2013, he launched his own app called "Viva Ronaldo" so that his millions of fans can share pictures and videos and take part in discussions about the Portugal captain.

Right: Ronaldo's popularity is shown by the millions of replica shirts that have been sold across the globe.

Ronaldo has repaid his fans many times for their support. In January 2014 he invited a young Real Madrid supporter suffering from cancer to watch a game at the Bernabeu in his own VIP box and in March he agreed to pay £70,000 for another young fan to undergo life-saving brain surgery. The Portugal star may have come a long way since he grew up in Funchal, but he will never forget his fans.

Above: Ronaldo makes a Portugal fan's dreams come true by handing him his game shirt after the Euro 2008 match against the Czech Republic.

GREAT PORTUGAL GOALS

The all-time leading scorer for his country, Ronaldo has hit some unbelievable wonder goals while on international duty for his beloved Portugal.

PORTUGAL 7 RUSSIA 1
WORLD CUP QUALIFIER, OCTOBER 13, 2004

There was a stunned silence inside the stadium in Lisbon when Ronaldo scored this wonder goal. He collected the ball just inside enemy territory and, when faced with five Russian defenders, blasted a fierce, dipping drive from outside the area into the top corner.

DENMARK 2 PORTUGAL 1
EURO 2012 QUALIFIER, OCTOBER 11, 2011

His greatest free-kick for his country, this 40-yard effort had everything – power, swerve and dramatic dip at the end. The ball flew just under the crossbar and into the net.

PORTUGAL 6 BOSNIA & HERZEGOVINA 2
EURO 2012 PLAYOFF, NOVEMBER 15, 2011

Another great example of his balance and technique, Ronaldo's second goal of the night came when he raced between the two central defenders and then left the helpless keeper stranded with a clever twist, finishing it all off with his weaker left foot.

Below: Pauleta leaps on Ronaldo's shoulders after another goal in the 2004 rout of Russia.

Above: Dutch goalkeeper Maarten Stekelenburg is helpless as Ronaldo scores one of his two goals to help Portugal reach the Euro 2012 quarter-finals.

NETHERLANDS 1 **PORTUGAL 2**

EURO 2012 GROUP B, JUNE 17, 2012

Ronaldo's two goals fired Portugal into the quarter-finals and his second was a work of art. Collecting a pass from Nani, he dummied a shot that left Dutch defender Gregory van der Wiel on his backside before driving low into the net.

SWEDEN 2 **PORTUGAL 3**

WORLD CUP PLAY-OFF, NOVEMBER 19, 2013

One of Ronaldo's greatest games for Portugal, his hat-trick booked the team's place in the World Cup Finals. His third goal was a belter as he glided into the Sweden penalty area, expertly took the ball past the goalkeeper and calmly stroked the ball home.

Above: Ronaldo celebrates after scoring his great goal against Bosnia & Herzegovina in 2011.

Below: The Swedish defence is powerless to stop the striker scoring another wonder goal in the 2014 World Cup qualifying playoff.

47

WORLD TRAVELLER

Wherever he goes on the planet, Ronaldo is sure to make headlines and is always guaranteed a warm welcome from his fans.

It is a good job that Ronaldo is not a nervous flyer because the superstar has clocked up thousands of miles in the air since he flew to England to sign for Manchester United back in 2003. There are few countries that he has not yet visited as a Real Madrid player, Portugal captain, charity ambassador or holidaymaker.

Modern footballers travel huge distances to play games and Ronaldo has been as far afield as China with Real Madrid for pre-season tours before returning to Spain for La Liga action.

Real Madrid traditionally set up camp in the USA every summer to get the squad ready for the new season and it was in 2013 that Ronaldo caught up with David Beckham in Los Angeles, a meeting of two of the most famous players in the history of the game.

Being part of the Portugal set-up has also seen the striker adding to his air miles, and during his record-breaking international career he has played throughout Europe as well as Israel, South Africa and Brazil.

Below: (from left) Ronaldo, Iker Casillas and David Beckham during an airport stopover on Madrid's preseason tour to the United States.

But it is not just football that sees Ronaldo reaching for his passport. The star represents a number of charities and in 2013 he made the journey to Indonesia in his role as an ambassador for the Mangrove Care Forum, an organisation that protects the natural environment in the country.

In the same year he also visited a secondary school in Singapore to support the launch of a new scholarship scheme for talented young athletes.

His football and charity work means Ronaldo has a hectic schedule, but there is still time for holidays with his son, Cristiano Junior, and family. In recent years, the striker has jetted off to Miami, the Maldives, Thailand, Ibiza and St Tropez to get away from it all.

Below: Ronaldo soaks up some rays while on a well-earned holiday.

Above: Ronaldo gets ready to get on another flight with the Portugal national team.

EUROPEAN SUPERSTAR

The Champions League is the biggest club competition on the planet and Ronaldo has been ripping it up in the tournament for 12 years.

Cristiano Ronaldo made his Champions League debut for Manchester United against Stuttgart on October 10, 2003, and has gone on to enjoy a remarkable love affair with European football's premier club tournament.

His breakthrough season in the competition came in the 2007–08 season. United had lost in the semi-finals the previous year, but with Ronaldo in sensational form they made it all the way to the Final to face Chelsea in Moscow, the capital of Russia.

Ronaldo had already scored seven goals on the way to the big match and he was on target again in Russia with an unstoppable first-half header that set up a penalty shootout after extra-time. United held their nerve to be crowned European champions for a third time in the club's history. Ronaldo's haul of eight goals made him the tournament's top scorer.

The striker's next great Champions League season came in 2012–13, when he once again finished as top scorer. Ronaldo fired in an incredible 12 goals, including two in a 3–2 last-16 win over United, as Real Madrid made it to the semi-finals for a second year running.

Ronaldo's form in the 2013–14 tournament was even better. He scored nine goals in the group stages, including a hat-trick against Galatasaray, and seven more in the knockout phase as Madrid marched into the Final to face city rivals Atletico Madrid.

The Final in Lisbon saw Real taken into extra-time by Atletico, but Ronaldo was on target from the penalty spot to seal a famous 4–1 win and secure the second Champions League winner's medal of his amazing career. In total, the striker scored 17 goals in just 11 games – moving to second all-time on the Champions Legaue – as Real ruled Europe for a record 10th time.

Real may have lost out to Juventus in the semi-finals of the 2014–15 competition, but it was still a record-breaking campaign for Ronaldo. In February 2015, in the last-16 match against Schalke, he became the first person in the competition's history to score in 12 consecutive away matches. When he netted against Juventus in the first leg of the semi-final, he joined Lionel Messi as the competition's all-time leading goalscorer (with 77 goals).

Above: Manchester United's team photo before the 2008 Champions League final against Chelsea.

Below: Ronaldo converts a penalty as Real defeat Juventus 2–1 in the 2013–14 Champions League.

Above: Ronaldo, who scored in Real's 4–1 win over neighbours Atletico in 2014, shows off the Champions League trophy after becoming one of the few players to be a winner with two clubs.

51

RONALDO AND HIS COACHES

The world's greatest footballer has played for some of the game's finest managers during his record-breaking career.

SIR ALEX FERGUSON

The man who brought him to Manchester United in 2003, Ferguson was a massive influence on Ronaldo's early career. Ferguson was the man who first switched Ronaldo from the wing to striker. Ronaldo then helped the Red Devils win a hat-trick of Premier League titles and the Champions League.

"I HAVE NOTHING BUT PRAISE FOR THE BOY. HE IS EASILY THE BEST PLAYER IN THE WORLD. HIS CONTRIBUTION AS A GOAL THREAT IS UNBELIEVABLE. HIS STATS ARE INCREDIBLE. STRIKES AT GOAL, ATTEMPTS ON GOAL, RAIDS INTO THE PENALTY BOX, HEADERS. IT IS ALL THERE. ABSOLUTELY ASTOUNDING."

Sir Alex Ferguson

JOSE MOURINHO

The two Portuguese teamed up with spectacular results at Real Madrid between 2010 and 2013 and with the duo together at the Bernabeu, Madrid toppled Barcelona as La Liga champions. Mourinho's famous management skills got the very best out of Ronaldo.

"IF MESSI IS THE BEST ON THE PLANET, RONALDO IS THE BEST IN THE UNIVERSE."

Jose Mourinho

LUIZ FELIPE SCOLARI

The Brazilian was Portugal's manager when he handed Ronaldo his international debut in 2003. The following year, the team reached the Euro 2004 Final. The pair worked together for four more years and thanks to Scolari's expertise and experience, Ronaldo matured into one of the game's most feared players.

"FOR ME HE IS THE BEST GUY IN THE WORLD TO WORK WITH. HE'S ALWAYS READY, ALWAYS TRYING HIS BEST AND IS ALWAYS LOOKING TO TRY SOMETHING DIFFERENT."

Luiz Felipe Scolari

CARLO ANCELOTTI

Another manager at Madrid, the famous Italian has won the league title in Italy, England and France and Ronaldo grew even more under his leadership. Ancelotti gave the Portuguese star plenty of freedom to attack and Ronaldo responded with some amazing performances for Real.

"RONALDO IS A UNIQUE PLAYER FOR ALL OF HIS TALENT AND HIS PROFESSIONALISM. HE IS A PLAYER WHO IS EXTRAORDINARY."

Carlo Ancelotti

GLOBAL SUPERSTAR

An ambassador for some of the world's biggest brands and the face of Pro Evolution Soccer, Ronaldo even has his own line of clothing and a museum dedicated to him.

Football is the most popular sport on the planet and it's no surprise that its greatest player is known all around the world. The striker may be a hero in his native Portugal, but he's just as famous in Peru, the Philippines and Poland.

"All around the world I have to deal with my fame," Ronaldo said. "I can't go anywhere without being recognised, which can be very hard."

His global reputation has seen the star sign lucrative sponsorship deals with Coca-Cola, men's fashion company Emporio Armani, Motorola and KFC and he has appeared in a series of TV adverts for sportswear giants Nike which have been broadcast all over the world.

In 2006 Ronaldo opened a fashion store called "CR7" (his trademarked initials and shirt number) on the island of Madeira and two years later he set up a second shop in the Portuguese capital Lisbon.

In December 2013 Ronaldo launched a museum, the "Museu CR7", in his hometown of Funchal to celebrate his amazing career. Thousands of fans from all over the world flocked to see the trophies, medals and memorabilia on show, underlining the strength of his global popularity.

The following month he was named the Grand Officer of the Order of Prince Henry by the Portuguese President, an exclusive honour that showed the impact Ronaldo has made in his own country.

The superstar was also honoured by the world famous Madame Tussauds in London when they unveiled a waxwork of him ahead of the 2010 FIFA World Cup. Ronaldo attended the opening ceremony in person with fellow footballers David Beckham, Pele and Steven Gerrard.

But perhaps the clearest sign of his fame is Ronaldo's impact on social media. His Facebook page is incredibly popular and his Twitter account has an astonishing number of followers. In May 2014, the international sports marketing company Repucom named him the most marketable football player on the planet.

Right: Ronaldo greets the President of Portugal in Lisbon in 2014 when he received his country's equivalent of a knighthood.

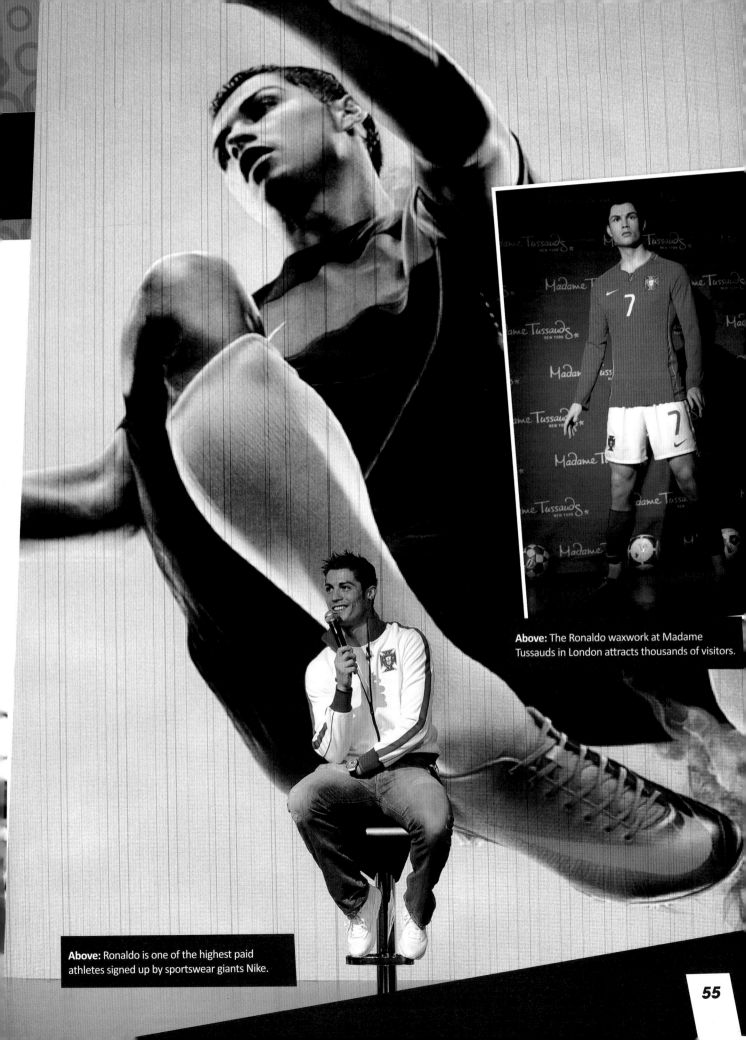

Above: The Ronaldo waxwork at Madame Tussauds in London attracts thousands of visitors.

Above: Ronaldo is one of the highest paid athletes signed up by sportswear giants Nike.

RECORD BREAKER

Ronaldo has smashed countless records and reached many marvellous milestones for both club and country during his fabulous career.

Above: Ronaldo celebrates becoming Portugal's all-time leading goalscorer (with 49) after netting a double against Cameroon in March 2014.

Ronaldo is Portugal's top scorer of all time and set the new record with two goals in a friendly against Cameroon in March 2014. This double strike took him to 49 for his country and past the 47-goal mark set by Pauleta.

The striker shares the record for the most goals scored in a 38-game Premier League season, hitting the back of the net 31 times in 2007–08. Alan Shearer, for Blackburn in 1995–96, and Luis Suarez, in 2013–14, also scored 31 goals.

Ronaldo scores 15 Champions League goals for Real in 2013, the record for goals in one calendar year in the competition. His 17 goals in 2013–14 also set a new mark for a season.

The Portuguese set a new record as the first player ever to score in six successive "El Clasico" games between Real Madrid and Barcelona. His amazing run began in the Copa del Rey in January 2012 and carried on until the two teams met in La Liga in October. The remarkable run brought seven goals in six appearances.

Ronaldo has rewritten the record books since he signed for Real Madrid and he is now the fastest player in the club's history to reach the 50, 100, 150 and 200 league goal milestones. He is also the quickest player to reach 200 goals in La Liga history.

The striker jointly holds the record for finding the back of the net in successive Champions League games, scoring in six games in a row for Real Madrid in the competition. His hot streak started with a 4–1 win over Ajax in December 2012 and after finding the back of the net home and away against both Manchester United and Galatasaray (to reach five games in a row), he made it six on the bounce with a goal in the first leg of the semi-final against Borussia Dortmund.

The star was in unstoppable form in front of goal for Madrid in the 2011–12 season, scoring a club record 60 goals for the side in all competitions.

Above: Ronaldo's double in Real's 3–0 win over Granada in September 2012 – it was his 149th league appearance – made him the quickest player in club and La Liga history to net 150 goals.

WHAT NEXT FOR RONALDO?

He has already achieved so much in more than a decade as a professional footballer but the ambitious Ronaldo never gets tired of success.

Although he celebrated his 30th birthday in 2015, Ronaldo is fitter, stronger and even hungrier for success today than the teenager who first broke into the Sporting Lisbon team back in 2002. Nobody knows how many more records he will break and how many more trophies he will lift before he hangs up his boots.

His incredible form in recent seasons led to rumours of a possible transfer to another big European club, but Real Madrid were quick to make it clear that their star player was going nowhere, offering the Portuguese magician a new extended contract that keeps him at the Bernabeu until 2018.

It means the Madrid fans can look forward to many more seasons watching Ronaldo's genius.

"This is my home, my family is here and I am really happy here," he said after signing the new deal in 2013. "But I respect all the clubs who have knocked at the door to ask something about me.

"The future nobody knows, but I just want to win trophies for this club and I appreciate that the fans still like me a lot to be here. I just want to do my best on the pitch with my goals, my assists and to try and help my team-mates."

There is also the big question of the Madrid captaincy. He first led out the team in January 2013 against Real Sociedad, but the Portuguese would love to be the full-time skipper.

At international level, Ronaldo is still dreaming of lifting the World Cup or European Championship and is desperate to inspire his country to glory. "I will only be fully content with my career when I have lifted a trophy with Portugal," he said before Euro 2012.

He also wants to become Portugal's most-capped player and beat Luis Figo's record of 127 international appearances. Only serious injury will stop him making that dream come true.

Below: The striker is all smiles after winning his 100th cap for Portugal in 2012.

Right: Ronaldo scored twice in January 2013 when he captained Madrid against Real Sociedad.

Above: Ronaldo and Real Madrid president Florentino Perez, the man who offered the superstar a new contract.

QUIZ TIME

Here are 20 questions to test just how much you know about Cristiano Ronaldo. All the answers can be found in the preceding pages of this book.

1 On which Portuguese island was Ronaldo born in 1985?
2 What did Ronaldo's mother Maria do for a living?
3 What was the name of the first amateur team he played for as an eight-year-old?
4 How many goals did Ronaldo score on his league debut for Sporting Lisbon?
5 What number shirt did he wear in his one season playing for Sporting Lisbon?
6 How much did Manchester United pay to sign Ronaldo from Sporting Lisbon in 2003?
7 Which player wore the number seven shirt at Old Trafford before Ronaldo joined the club?
8 Against which team did the player make his Champions League debut for United in October 2003?
9 Name the manager who gave Ronaldo his international debut in 2003?
10 Against which country did Ronaldo score the winning penalty in the 2006 World Cup quarter-final?

Above: See question 5. Ronaldo made his name for Sporting Lisbon wearing which shirt number?

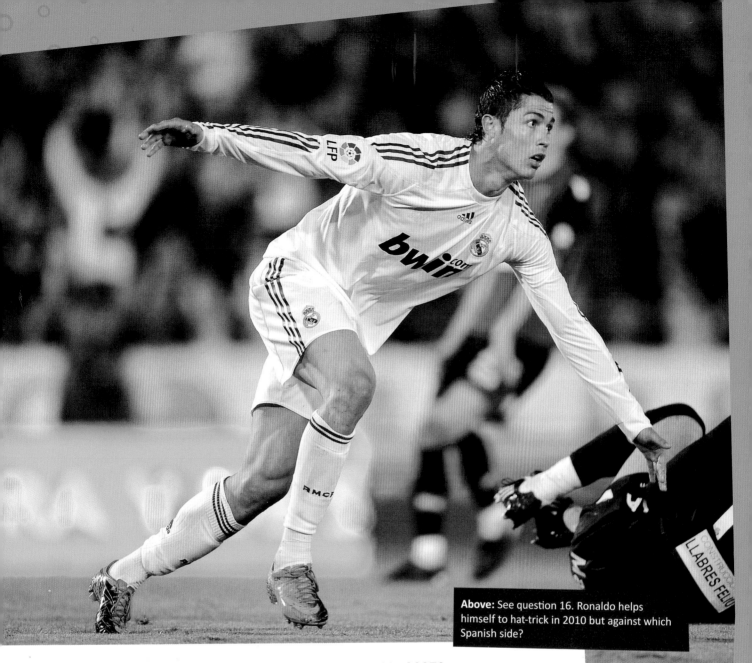

Above: See question 16. Ronaldo helps himself to hat-trick in 2010 but against which Spanish side?

11 Against which team did Ronaldo first captain Portugal in 2007?

12 How many goals did he score during the 2007–08 Premier League season when Manchester United were crowned champions?

13 Against which team did he score a 40-yard screamer in 2009 to win the first-ever FIFA Puskas Award for the best goal of the year?

14 How many fans were in the Bernabeu stadium to welcome the Portuguese when he signed for Real Madrid in 2009?

15 In which two years was Ronaldo named in the European Championship Team of the Tournament?

16 Against which team did the striker score his first hat-trick for Real Madrid in 2010?

17 How many league goals did he score for Madrid in 2010–11 to win the European Golden Shoe for a second time?

18 Against which country did Ronaldo win his 100th cap for Portugal in a World Cup qualifier in 2012?

19 How many times has the star been named in the FIFA FIFPro World XI?

20 When Ronaldo scored against Juventus in the first leg of the 2014–15 Champions League semi-final, he became, alongside Lionel Messi, the competition's all-time leading goalscorer. How many goals has he scored in the Champions League?

ANSWERS – SEE PAGE 63

PICTURE QUIZ

Cristiano Ronaldo is no stranger to getting his hands on silverware but can you spot which trophies the star is holding in these pictures? The answers are on the opposite page.

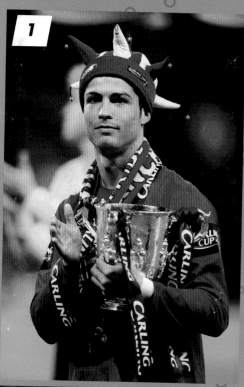